FAITH, HOPE AND LOVE
An Inspiration Through Troubled Times

Sandra Nairen

Eloquent Books

Copyright © 2010
All rights reserved – Sandra Nairen

No part of this book may be reproduced or transmitted in any form or by any means, graphic, electronic, or mechanical, including photocopying, recording, taping, or by any information storage retrieval system, without the permission, in writing, from the publisher.

Eloquent Books
An imprint of Strategic Book Group
P. O. Box 333
Durham, CT 06422
www.StrategicBookGroup.com

ISBN: 978-1-60911-740-5

Printed in the United States of America

Book Design: Judy Maenle

I would like to dedicate this book
to all those people who have supported me
and encouraged me in my writing
and helped me see my dream
of becoming a published
poet fulfilled.

Contents

As We Look at the News Each Day	1
Don't Worry About Tomorrow	2
We Need Patience	4
Jesus Loves Us As We Are	5
As We Come to the Time of Lent	7
When Jesus Called the First Disciples	8
Valentine's Day	9
If We Could Look into the Eyes of Jesus	10
Jesus' Hands	11
When Things Are Imperfect	12
In the Garden	13
When You're Having a Really Bad Day	15
God Does His Miracles and Wonders	16
Time Ticks Away	18
The 23rd Psalm	19
Every Morning I Am Blessed	21
Spring, Summer, Winter and Fall	23
Sow the Seed	25
Put On the Armour of God	26
You Broke the Bread	27
A Place Prepared in Heaven	28
Life Is Like a Jigsaw Puzzle	29
Why?	30
Watch Out for the Traffic Lights	31
Palm Sunday	32
Don't Feel Like Good Friday	33
The Seasons of Life	34
Blue Sky	35

Tears of Sorrow for Joy	36
How Lucky We Are	37
There May Be Rain	38
Be Like the Eagle	39
The Lord Is My Shepherd	40
Hold On to Your Dream	41
Holy Angels	42
The Lord Is Patient	43
The Heart	45
When Your Purse Is Empty	46
When You Feel Down and Sad	47
We Have to Have Sunshine as Well as Rain	48
When Your Card Is Declined	49
You Are Special	50
When You Feel Unloved	51
Life Is Like a Seesaw	52
Faith, Hope, and Love	53
Jesus the Vine	54
The Crown	55
When It Is Your Birthday	56
Life Is Not a Fairy Tale	57
At the Break of Day	58
Let Your Face Shine	59
Money Cannot Bring Happiness	60
God Sent the Holy Spirit	61
Two Paths	62
Give Us Inspiration	63
How Beautiful the Flowers Are	64
We Don't Need Designer Clothes	65
How Beautiful Are the Lilies	66

Sometimes Life Is Unfair	67
Life Is Like a Painting	68
Don't Let the Sun Go Down on Your Anger	69
How Lovely It Is in the Summer	70
When Your Burdens Grow Too Heavy	71
You May Speak in Tongues	72
When You Feel Like Job	73
Thank God in Times of Suffering	74
Dry Your Tears	75
The Phone Call	76
God Has No Concept of Time	77
Every Cloud Has a Silver Lining	78
Written On the Palm of God's Hand	79
You Need a Firm Anchor	80
We Look at the Sun and Moon	81
Hope	82
When You Are Having a Bad Day	83
He Will Fill Your Mouth with Laughter	84
When the Light Seems Dim	85
When the News Can Be Full of Gloom	86
Feeling Cold and Empty	87
Say Good Morning	88
I Believe	89
When Creation Began	90
Advent	91
Do You Ever Wonder	92
As the Sunshine Melts the Snow	93
Chase the Clouds Away	94
The Rainbow	95
Free As a Bird	96

Thoughts of Summer	97
Look At the Seasons	98
The Light of Christ	99
Spring	100
Winter	101
Easter	102
Three Crosses	103
Do You Ever Think of Christmas	104
Christmas	105
The Ultimate Sacrifice	106
Angels	107

As We Look at the News Each Day

As we read the papers,
  And turn the page,
We see conflict and murder,
Theft and rage,
Tragedies where people die,
The question we humans ask is,
"Please, God, tell us why?"

He is not to blame for what we see,
But Adam letting in sin,
When he ate the fruit of the tree,
The world was perfect,
And just meant to be,
Until we spoiled it,
People like you and me.

We have a hope,
Through this world of dismay,
As we have a Saviour,
Who will light the way,
To a better future for you and me,
If we only turn to him and trust him,
The good around we will see.

Don't Worry About Tomorrow

You sometimes worry,
About the small things in life,
Which can add extra burdens,
To everyday life.
Such as what to do for dinner today,
Or why your colleague ignored you,
As you said "Hello" on the way.
Then, before you know it,
The problems like a hill,
With an uphill struggle,
Which can sometimes make you ill.

So don't worry about tomorrow,
For God will take care of the day,
And you will feel happier,
In a more positive way,
You will feel more certain,
Of the future ahead,
And no tossing and turning,
Worrying in your bed.

So cast your burdens upon Jesus,
Take them to him in prayer,
For Jesus is master of all he surveys,
And of your problems he'll really take care.

We sometimes end up in a valley,
Where we feel down in despair,
We sometimes end up on a mountain top,
Happy and without a care.

Whatever our situation,
However we may feel,
Jesus is always there for us,
His love for you is real.

We Need Patience

Sometimes we need the patience of Job,
To see us through the day,
Patience is a virtue,
Sometimes people do say.
Patience comes through trusting God,
Who acts when the time is right,
When the tunnel is dark and there seems no hope
There is always a glimmer of light.

Job lost his children,
And all his riches too,
But he never gave up praising God,
And neither should you,
For God truly blessed him,
With more than he had before,
As he just kept on praising God,
Who blessed him more and more.

God will never burden us,
With more than we can stand,
He knows how much we can take,
And with his mighty hand,
He will take away our troubles,
And disperse them one by one,
Until our despair turns to joy,
And we can feel that life is fun.

Jesus Loves Us As We Are

Jesus loves us with our defects,
Just the way we are,
And in this world of darkness,
We should shine just like a star.
In this materialistic world,
Of take instead of give,
We should show by example,
By the way in which we live.
We should dare to be different,
In what we do and what we say,
Despite the obstructions,
That may stand in our way.
The obstruction of trying to please others,
In case we could offend,
Instead of pleasing God above,
Who is more than just a friend.

Jesus came for sinners,
Just like you and me,
And whatever sin we have committed,
We know that we are free,
Remember on the cross,
With thieves upon each side,
He said to the one who truly believed,
"In paradise you will abide."

People will not like the way we are different,
And sometimes leave us out,
But isn't that part of the Christian way,
And what being a Christians about?
Jesus himself was an outcast,
Excluded by his own,
But when he went back to Heaven,
He took his royal throne.

So cling on to the hope,
That one day we will see,
The face of Jesus smiling,
When at home in Heaven we'll be.

As We Come to the Time of Lent

As we come to the time of Lent,
   Let us think of our sins and repent,
   Let us say sorry for what we have done,
   Ask forgiveness through God's blessed son.
We need to feel loved and forgiven,
To make us feel more whole,
To make us feel happier within ourselves,
And to feel a cleansing of the soul.

Jesus although he was tempted,
Never gave up or gave in,
He is the spotless Lamb of God,
Who laid down his life for our sin.

Not only in Lent,
But each day of the year,
We should ask God's forgiveness,
But we need not fear,
For his love is without ending,
It stretches forever,
It's a love so strong,
That nothing can sever.
As we come to a time of repentance,
And once again think of our sin,
Ask Jesus to give you a brand new start,
And peace that is only through him.

When Jesus Called the First Disciples

When Jesus called the first disciples,
   Simon, Andrew, James, and John,
They all left the jobs they were doing,
   To follow God's own son.
Jesus had such a command and power,
   In all he did and said,
With his parables and miracles,
   Such as raising Lazarus from the dead.

We too have a duty to follow,
   And wherever it may be heard,
Tell others of Jesus, our Saviour,
   We should go and spread the word.

It may be in the workplace,
   It may be on the train,
It may be on the bus,
   Or even on a plane.

We are here to gather the harvest,
   It is ready to gather in,
Just be like John the Baptist,
   Tell others to repent of their sin.

Tell others there is hope in Jesus,
   He is the only way,
To a whole new life here on Earth,
   And a home in Heaven one day.

Valentine's Day

Today is Valentine's day,
The day we declare our love,
But we don't need chocolates and flowers,
For we have God's love from above.
It's a love that's unlike an earthly love,
A love that will not fade,
A love that knows no earthly bounds,
And only in Heaven is made.

We know we have his special love,
A love that knows no end,
For he is our faithful companion,
A very special friend.

He will never break our heart,
Or leave us torn in two,
For his love is greater than we can take in,
He sent his son for you.

His son showed his love for all people,
Whoever they may be,
But his final act of love for all,
Was his death on Calvary.

If We Could Look into the Eyes of Jesus

If we could look into the eyes of Jesus,
 They would look into our soul,
 He can cleanse us from all our sins,
 And truly make us whole.

His eyes are full of compassion,
His eyes are full of love,
For we know we are truly blessed,
As those eyes look down from above.

Those eyes will cry when we are in pain,
And when we are feeling sad,
They also laugh along with us,
When we are happy and glad.

So if we could look into the eyes of Jesus,
And we could look upon his face,
We would see a face that is full of compassion,
A face that is full of grace.

Jesus' Hands

Jesus' hands were skilled at the plane,
He used his hands to cure the lame,
Before life on Earth,
He created the night,
And with those hands,
He created the light,
And with those hands,
He created the sea,
And not forgetting,
Those hands created you and me.
With those same hands,
He bore the nails of pain,
And with those hands,
He took away our shame.
Those hands created the moon and sun,
And prayed in the garden, "Your will be done."
He still uses those hands,
We can see it each day,
As the sun rises and sets,
And the world spins on its way.

When Things Are Imperfect

When things are imperfect or rotten,
   We throw them in the bin,
   But unlike us human beings,
   God doesn't think we're passed it,
   Because of wrong doing and sin.

We can easily throw away some food,
   Or clothes we no longer need,
   But God looks down on each of us,
   As a little tiny seed,
   One that needs love and protection,
   One that he tends with love,
   One that will flourish and grow each day,
   With his guidance from above.

So God sent a great redeemer,
   Who cleanses us from our sin,
   And when we ask for forgiveness,
   He gives us peace and wholeness within,

So next time you go to the tip,
   Or put something in the bin,
   Remember you're not like the rubbish,
   Useless and no good to him.

In the Garden

You prayed in the garden while the others slept,
  You knelt before your Father and silently wept,
  You knew the path that lay ahead,
  And by the following evening you would be dead.

Through the garden in the night,
You could see the soldiers coming,
Carrying their light.
The betrayer kissed you on the cheek,
But hardly a word in your defence,
Did you speak.

They led away God's holy lamb,
To be slaughtered for the sins of man,
How you must have felt,
We will never know,
But you died for us,
Because you loved us so.

Before the cock crowed three times,
Your disciple Peter denied,
The crowd they shouted, "Crucify!"
And on the cross you died.

But that was not the end of it,
On the third day you arose,
You appeared to your disciples,
The ones you specially chose.

You finally went back to Heaven,
On what is known as Ascension Day,
And because of your love,
And your death on the cross,
We'll meet in Heaven one day.

When You're Having a Really Bad Day

When you're having a really bad day,
You're late for work,
And the kids disobey.
Just remember that good,
Will follow the bad,
That happiness will follow,
When you're feeling sad,
That grey skies will finally turn to blue,
And things will turn out better,
Just for you.

You know you can turn to God,
He is there to help you,
As you sometimes wonder,
Why you are going through,
This time of trouble,
And times of trial,
Just be patient and wait awhile.

Don't give up,
Just look to the sky,
And see the clouds as they float by,
Just like the clouds,
Your troubles will be gone,
And a rainbow will appear,
And so will the sun.

God Does His Miracles and Wonders

When you read your Bible,
 There we can see,
 How down through the ages,
 God did miracles and wonders,
 For ordinary people like you and me.

He took Moses and made him a leader,
He led the Israelites across the Red Sea,
He took David the shepherd boy,
And when Goliath he did see,
He did not flinch or say, "I can't."
The giant he did slay,
And even now in this present time,
We see miracles day by day,
There are people who are cured of cancer,
Who thought they'd never see the day,
They'd get the all clear from the hospital,
As they have suffered along the way.

We don't have to be rich or powerful,
Or sit upon a throne,
For we belong to God above,
We are his very own.

The disciples were ordinary people,
From Jesus they heard the call,
And when he said, "Follow me,"
They left their homes and gave their all,
To follow the master,
In whose presence they did stand,
Then they spread the good news of Jesus,
As he did command.

We are also his disciples,
And we should follow, too,
And spread the good news of Jesus,
To places old and new.
So go and tell your relatives,
And go and tell your friends,
That Jesus is the good news,
With a love that never ends.

Time Ticks Away

Time ticks away,
As we go on each day,
Life can seem so boring,
As we go along our way.
Each day we go about,
Doing exactly just the same,
In our humdrum lives,
That just seems so mundane.
Monday to Friday,
The alarm does sound,
You jump out of bed,
Your feet touch the ground,
You get breakfast ready,
The children to school,
Someone says something,
To make you lose your cool.
But having Jesus in our lives,
We can feel happiness within,
And filled with the Holy Spirit,
A bubbling will begin,
A bubbling of happiness,
One we can't contain,
One that helps us through life's trials,
And one that will remain.
We will finally feel some peace and hope,
A joy that comes from within,
When you ask him into your life,
You will finally begin,
To see what you've missed out on,
And you'll be sorry you didn't before,
Take that step of answering the knock,
And opening the door.

The 23rd Psalm

As we read the 23rd psalm,
We read how God will keep us from harm,
All our needs will be met,
So we need not fret,
Our Lord is the small voice of calm.

As through the dark valley we walk,
To our Lord God we can talk,
With God on high,
We can reach for the sky,
Nothing will he deny.
Unless it is not his will,
Or he knows it's not good,
It's for ill,
Then he will say no,
Then the correct way he'll show,
And show us which way to go.

To pastures green he will lead,
And at his table we will feed,
Our cup will overflow,
As the love for our Lord does grow.

Though evil may abound,
We stand on holy ground,
Our Lord from evil he'll keep,
And watch over us,
By day and in sleep,
So do not fear what's to be,
For the Lord will protect thee.

King David wrote this wonderful psalm,
When his enemies attacked,
And meant him harm,
And so we can face whatever will be,
Knowing God is our protector,
And forever we'll see,
How he cares and protects us,
And will meet all our needs,
As each day he provides,
Clothes us and feeds.

Every Morning I Am Blessed

Every morning I am blessed
By God's love and grace,
I am caressed,
I do not know,
What lies ahead,
As I finally struggle,
To get out of bed.
There is one thing that I know,
How much God loves me so,
He proves it every day I live,
With every blessing,
That he gives.

The blessing of life,
The birds that sing,
A rainbow in the sky,
Life's simple things,
Such as the beauty of nature,
At what it says,
Of how bountiful God is,
In many ways.
The blessing of our family,
The blessing of our friends,
The blessing of being a child of God,
On whom we can depend.

I know I'm not worthy,
But still the blessings never end,
And at the end of the day,
I thank him,
For being my best friend,
For the way he has watched,

My every move,
And his love for me he forever proves,
By sending his son who shed his blood,
For sinners like myself,
To make me good.

Spring, Summer, Winter and Fall

The summer has gone,
And the autumn is here,
And so it is with the seasons of life,
Each time they do appear.
We have happy times like summer,
When the sun always seem to shine,
Everything is perfect,
And all seems sublime.

Then autumn follows,
The leaves come tumbling down,
All cascading in different shades,
Of yellow, red, and brown,
Just like when our lives seem wrong,
It seems to fall apart,
When things don't go just as planned,
And you ache within your heart.

Then winter comes with rain, wind and snow,
When we are blown about,
And don't know which way to go,
Our lives are so cold, so empty and bleak,
It is then more than ever,
The Lord we seek.
For when we feel down,
And in deep despair,
We know the Lord is always there,
To turn our darkness into glorious light,
When things will turn out better,
And turn out just right.

The comes the spring with its hope anew,
The shoots appear new life for me and you,
We think of Easter and all that it means,
To have Jesus as our Saviour,
To help us fulfil our dreams.

So we are back to summer and the sky of azure blue,
Just thank the Lord, our Saviour,
And what he has done for you.

Sow the Seed

Sow the seed of happiness,
As you go through the day,
Sow the seed of happiness,
As you go on your way,
For as you give a cheerful smile,
Or do a kindly deed,
You could be sowing the seed of happiness,
To a hurting soul in need.

You could have sown the seed of happiness,
And even before you know,
They could pass it on to someone else,
The seed will grow and grow.

Wouldn't it be a wonderful world,
If the seed were to be scattered around,
Nurtured with peace and love,
And firmly rooted in the ground.

Put On the Armour of God

Put on the armour of God,
   From your head to your toes be shod,
   With the full protection of he,
   Who died on Calvary.

With the belt of truth round your waist,
And the breastplate of righteousness in place,
No evil on earth can stand,
As you are in God's hand.

With the shoes of righteousness on your feet,
You will defeat any problem you meet,
It will give you the peace from within,
And the victory over evil you'll win.

With the sword of God in your hand,
With the word of God you will stand,
Despite what others do or say,
You will be fully protected each day.

You Broke the Bread

You broke the bread,
   You took the cup,
   You knew the painful road ahead,
   But you never gave up.

In the garden,
You knelt to pray,
"Not my will, but yours be done,"
The ever-faithful,
Obedient son.

The disciples deserted you,
Denied you and ran,
Scared of the authorities,
Frightened of man.

Let us remember each Sunday,
When to your alter we come,
In awe and wonder,
Of what you have done.

As we do this each week,
In remembrance of him,
Who laid down his life,
An atonement for sin.

A Place Prepared in Heaven

Jesus went to Heaven,
 To prepare a place for you,
The room is free,
You don't even have to pay extra for the view.

For Jesus paid the fee on Calvary's tree,
The room is there to take,
So whatever we do in this life,
Whatever our mistake,
The room is there and ready,
And paid for by his blood,
He took all our sin and shame,
And in our place he stood.

When we get to Heaven,
We will have won the final race,
No more in shame we will be,
Or hold our head in disgrace.
For we will have won the crown of life,
A crown that will not fade,
All thanks to Jesus, our Saviour,
Who shed his blood to save.

Life Is Like a Jigsaw Puzzle

Life is like a jigsaw puzzle,
 Put together day by day,
 Sometimes there are azure skies,
 Sometimes they are grey.

Life is full of rainbows,
 Whenever there is rain,
 So look for the rainbow in the sky,
 Through trouble and through pain.

We sometimes feel pieces are missing,
 Or sometimes not quite right,
 That's when we put our faith in God,
 And trust with all our might.

So don't give up when things go wrong,
 And the pieces don't quite fit,
 For God will set your feet upon a rock,
 And pull you out of the pit.

Why?

Why does the sun come up,
   And the moon come out at night?
Why do the planets spin,
   And stars shine with a twinkling light?
It is all because of our Father God,
Who made the mighty sea,
And all because he loves us,
And in his image he made me.

Nothing in this universe just happened,
But is planned,
And in his mighty power,
Life springs at his command.

Each creature, plant, and baby born,
Heralds the beginning of a brand new dawn,
New life, new hope is all around,
When we open our ears to the sound,
Of joy and laughter,
And take to God our fears,
For he is the Lord and Master,
Of a millennium of years.

Watch Out for the Traffic Lights

When we are walking,
　Or travelling on the road,
We certainly have to observe,
The highway code.
When the lights are red,
It means no,
When the lights are green,
It's time to go.

So we should observe,
God's traffic lights,
To show what is wrong,
And to know what's right,
When they are red,
He means we could go astray,
But when he gives us,
The green light,
We know it's his way.

Sometimes we feel frustrated,
As we see a traffic jam,
Where all we hope and pray for,
Does not go according to plan.
Then we have to be patient,
And sit there in the queue,
And wait for God,
In his own time,
To show us what to do.

So always observe the traffic lights,
And always keep God's code,
You will know you are following God's rules,
And to a new life cross the road.

Palm Sunday

People waved their branches of palm,
  And welcomed you with open arms,
  They shouted, "Hosanna to God on high!"
When in less than a week,
They shouted, "Crucify!"

  You rode on a donkey into town,
No royal robe,
Or golden crown.
The high priests and leaders,
Told the crowd to be quiet,
For they were afraid of a riot.

What went wrong?
What was it about?
From Hosanna to God's son,
Then for your death,
They did shout.

In one more week,
Everyone would see,
Why this had to happen,
Why it had to be,
For through the cross,
And through the pain,
You were the spotless Lamb of God,
For sinners slain.

Don't Feel Like Good Friday

Don't feel like Good Friday,
Full of gloom and doom,
Just think of Easter Sunday,
And the joy of the empty tomb,
For when we have a problem,
We never are alone,
We can talk to God at anytime,
Just like picking up the phone.

His ears are always open,
To listen to our prayer,
And he sends his holy angels,
To protect us and to care,
Although we may not see the angels,
They are all around,
And when God hears our cry for help,
Guardian angels can be found.

So never ever be afraid,
Of what turns up in life,
For God will always give us strength,
Through troubles and through strife,
For nothing on this earth can sever,
God's love for me and you,
So just take your prayers to God,
And he will certainly bring you through.

The Seasons of Life

Sometimes our lives can feel like summer or spring,
  When the flowers bloom,
  And the birds do sing,
  But then the autumn and winter follow,
  When life seems unfair and sometimes hollow.

Take heart through the autumn and winter,
And count each day,
Till spring arrives,
And summer's on its way,
For through the dark of empty days,
Breaks forth the sunshine with its rays,
When life again,
Will be bathed in light,
You'll come through the darkness,
And into the light.

Blue Sky

Blue sky above me,
The sand beneath my feet,
The warmth of the summer sun,
Life can be so sweet.

Life is such a precious gift,
And should not be ignored,
So don't sit there feeling sad,
Or may be feeling bored.

Jesus gave his life to give us life,
So you should be ever grateful,
Just take him as your Lord and King,
And you'll find he's truly faithful.

Tears of Sorrow for Joy

You may cry tears of sorrow,
  But joy will come in the morning,
  This is a promise from the Lord,
  So as the day is dawning,
  Just dry your eyes and be glad,
  That today will be better,
  And don't feel sad.

You cannot alter what has been,
The future only by God can be seen,
Only he knows what's best,
And why we go through,
The troubles and turmoil,
Life may throw at you.

Just remember that you will survive,
And just count your blessings,
Each day you're alive,
God knows how you feel,
He will come to your aid,
Just trust him,
Have faith,
And you will not be dismayed.

How Lucky We Are

Food on the table,
  A roof over my head,
  Clothes for my body,
  A soft comfortable bed,
  I am richer than most,
  With all that I need,
  God's love to protect me,
  I am wealthy indeed.

  I don't need the trappings,
  Of glamour or fame,
  Who wants to be noticed?
  Who needs to know your name?
  For I am noticed,
  By Jesus, God's son,
  And there one day in Heaven,
  I will worship him,
  When my time on Earth is done.

There May Be Rain

There may be rain on the window pane
   But I have sunshine in my heart,
   I have Jesus in my life,
   So as the day does start,
   I pray that through the day,
   Whatever traps may be laid,
   That I will cope,
   With faith and hope,
   And never be afraid.

   Jesus is our friend and guide,
   Who with us will always abide,
   On him we always can depend,
   He'll be with us always,
   Until the very end,
   No only in this life,
   But through eternity,
   When finally he'll call us home,
   How happy we will be.

Be Like the Eagle

Be like the eagle,
  Who soars in the sky,
  The stronger the wind,
  The higher they fly.
  We can also soar,
  When things go wrong,
  God will see us through it,
  And make us strong.

We each go through trials,
And wonder why,
We sit and we sulk,
And often cry,
But we have a father,
Who cares for our well being,
And hates to see his children suffer,
And hurts at what he's seeing.
So next time you feel down and sad,
Remember that things are not that bad,
Remember the eagle in the sky,
How high it can soar,
Just give it a try.

The Lord Is My Shepherd

The Lord is my shepherd,
I shall not want,
I was christened,
A child of my Father God,
With holy water,
From a font.

My God parents took my vows,
As I was too young to talk,
But God knew my destiny,
Before I could even walk.

Now that I am older,
I decided on my own,
That I am proud,
To take Christ's name,
And let the fact be known.

I shout if from the rooftops,
For everyone to hear,
That the Lord is my shepherd,
And to him I am precious and dear.

Hold On to Your Dream

How dark the days of winter,
How cold and empty they seem,
Unless we remember the victory,
And hold on to your dream.

The victory over Satan,
When things seem dark and grey,
Can soon be turned to sunshine,
When we let Jesus have his way.

Whatever we are going through,
Is nothing to what you will see,
When you see the final breakthrough,
And the final victory.

So never give up on having hope,
And never give up on your dream,
For just like Joseph,
As we all know,
Things are not quite what they seem.

Holy Angels

Holy angels praise and worship,
 Round your throne,
 Each day and night,
 They watch over us and protect us,
 Showing us what is wrong and right.

Whenever sadness, temptation, trouble,
In our path and dangers lie,
They will come to help us through it,
Although they cannot be seen with the human eye.

We may not see these angels,
But they are always found,
In acts of deeds and kindness,
And love that's spread around.

So next time someone offers to help you,
In your hour of need,
Stretch out and take their helping hand,
Your hopes and dreams to succeed.

The Lord Is Patient

The Lord is a God,
  Of patience and justice,
  Slow to anger,
  And swift to bless,
  The very person,
  We can turn to,
  When our lives,
  Are in a mess.

We can always rely,
Upon his judgement,
And know that he will be,
Always there,
When we need him,
His miracles we'll see.

Life sometimes,
Seems so hopeless,
When things go from bad to worse,
But we can turn to Jesus,
Who will turn blessings from a curse.

Just like the story of Joseph,
When to Potiphar,
He was sold,
He went to prison,
Through no fault of his own,
And ended up,
Honoured with gold.

Everything is done for a purpose,
God always has a plan,
So just put your trust in Jesus Christ,
Who we know will do all he can.

The Heart

The heart is a vital organ,
It pumps the blood around,
It can flutter with love for others,
And where Jesus can be found.

If we ask Jesus into our lives,
And to abide within our heart,
We will see our lives changed completely,
And then we will see the start,
Of how we can look at others,
Our enemies we will love,
And our Father in Heaven,
Will smile on us,
And send blessings from above.

When we love each other,
As Jesus did,
He mixed with those in need,
We will follow his example,
And for the outcasts we will plead.

When Your Purse Is Empty

When your finances go from bad to worse,
   And you're left with an empty purse,
   Remember the widow with the mite,
   To the Lord don't hold your purse strings tight.

God has promised if we give,
We will have blessings and money,
As long as we live.
So give to the Lord,
When you are poor,
And the Lord will provide you,
With more and more,
Your cup will run over,
Pressed down with good measure,
And then in Heaven,
You will store your treasure.

When You Feel Down and Sad

When you are down in the valley,
   Look to the mountain top,
   The journey may be hard and dangerous,
   But climb and never stop.

The obstacles you come across,
The rocks upon the way,
Are all part of the trials of life,
We come across each day.

We sometimes feel tired and exhausted,
And on the point of giving up,
But we can turn to Jesus,
When things get really tough.

When we look up to the hills,
Where our strength comes from,
We pray to God and ask for help,
And let his will be done.

We Have to Have Sunshine as Well as Rain

We have to have the sunshine,
As well as sometimes rain,
We have to experience the highs in life,
As well as the lows and the pain.

Where would the flowers be,
If it were always bright,
With sunshine every minute,
And no rain or dew at night.

They would wither up and perish,
And dry without hope,
And so would we,
If we didn't have the Lord,
To give us strength to cope.

So just remember with the sun,
We have to have some rain,
To help us grow,
To give us life,
And let us live again.

When Your Card Is Declined

When you go to the till,
   And your card is declined,
   Jesus will never reject you,
   You are always on his mind.

You may be as poor as a church mouse,
With not much money to spend,
But you are richer beyond compare,
With Jesus as your friend.

Our riches and treasures,
Are not of this Earth,
But stored up in Heaven above,
With Jesus, our Saviour,
One day we'll be,
To sing of his glory and love.

You Are Special

You are special and unique,
From the hairs on your head,
To the tips of your feet.

No one on earth,
Ever will be,
Before or after,
Be quite like you and me.
You have been made,
By God's own hand,
And many blessings,
Have been bestowed,
At his command.

Each day that you live,
You should give him praise,
For all he has done,
Till the end of your days,
Then in Heaven,
You will be at home,
With the holy angels,
Around God's throne.

When You Feel Unloved

When you feel unloved and unwanted,
There is the Lord you can turn to,
For he loves you more than you know,
And he will comfort you,
Through the hurt and pain of sorrow,
The feeling of a broken heart,
For you can rely on your father above,
From him you will never depart.

He holds onto you tightly,
Never to let go,
And when the path you take is wrong,
The right way he will show.
You are like the sheep,
Who had gone astray,
The prodigal son,
He will not turn away.

You may turn your back on him,
With temptation and sin,
But he will gently guide you back,
And when you trust him completely,
Nothing will you lack.

Life Is Like a Seesaw

Life is like a seesaw,
  You feel up then you feel down,
It's no use feeling miserable,
Sitting wearing a frown,
For feeling sad or happy,
Surely you will find,
It's not a matter of how you feel,
But just a state of mind.

If you look on the bright side,
When all else is gloom and doom,
You will start to feel much happier,
Then you will find the room,
To smile again,
And be thankful,
For all the Lord has done,
And then life will feel much sweeter,
And your soul feels full of fun.

Faith, Hope, and Love

Faith, hope, and love,
Are God given from above.

Love is patient,
Love is kind,
Love is putting other first,
And having good thoughts in your mind.
Love is caring for your enemies,
As well as you friends,
And showing kindness,
Love and understanding,
That never ends.

Love is not being envious,
Boastful, or proud,
Love is shown in actions,
And saying out loud,
That you care for them and love them,
As Jesus did for you,
And shown through the way we live,
In all we say and do.

Faith and hope together,
Will see us through life's trials,
And turn our sadness into joy,
And turn our tears to smiles.
Although the three are important,
The greatest of these is love,
For when we truly love each other,
We are certainly blessed from above.

Jesus the Vine

Jesus is the vine,
 We are the branches,
 God is the gardener above,
 He prunes us daily,
 So we can bear fruit,
 And sprinkles us with love.

We should bear fruit,
 And spread the word,
 That God is good and just,
 It is our duty and our joy,
 To obey him and to trust.

We will be judged,
 By the fruit we bear,
 And so we must endeavour,
 To do the will,
 Of our Father above,
 Whose hold on us,
 No one can sever.

The Crown

The crown of thorns,
  Now turned to gold,
The greatest story,
  Ever told,
Of how you came,
  To Earth to save,
And willingly,
  Your life you gave.

You cared for those who others despised,
And looked at them with compassion,
In your eyes.
The outcasts, the sinners,
The lame the blind,
No one before,
Had been so kind.
You showed you cared,
And made them whole,
And in the process,
Saved their soul.

No one changed the world like you,
Our outlook on others,
You changed our view,
To love each other,
Is your command,
So let us do it,
With the help of God's hand.

When It Is Your Birthday

When it is your birthday,
   Don't feel sad and forlorn,
Just thank God,
For every new day,
Especially the day,
You were born.

With every year,
You grow in age,
You grow in blessings too,
For God will lead you,
Every day of your life,
And show you,
What to do.

If we truly have such faith,
And trust God's holy son,
We can look at life,
In a different way,
And see it can be fun.

Feeling sad and downcast,
Is not the way to be,
For if we look to Jesus,
How happy you will be,
For he can take your sorrow,
And put a smile back,
On your face,
Then you will to feel,
Full of joy,
And also feel his grace.

Life Is Not a Fairy Tale

Life is not a fairy tale,
With happy ever after,
Every day cannot be filled,
With fun, joy, and laughter.

Through this mortal life of ours,
We go through the refiner's fire,
We just have to pray to God,
To give us strength,
So that we'll never tire.

In our weakness,
We have strength,
For God is always there,
To strengthen and support us,
And he sends others,
To show they care.

At the Break of Day

At the break of day,
  When you awake,
  Give the day to God,
  And to him do take,
  All your cares and worries,
  Your problems, and shame,
  And ask him to help you,
  In Jesus' name.

At the end of the day,
When all is done,
Thank God for the day,
And all that he's done,
For he has watched,
And guided,
And shown you the way,
And loves you,
More than words can say.

Let Your Face Shine

Let your face shine,
   Like that of an angel,
   May you be a guiding light,
   May you turn your back,
   On what is wrong,
   And strive to do,
   What is right.

May you love your enemies,
   As a friend,
   With a concern and love,
   That knows no end,
   Just as our Father,
   Taught us too,
   For don't forget,
   He first loved you.

The love he shows,
   Comes as a flood,
   As did the shedding,
   Of Jesus's blood,
   For no greater love,
   Will ever be,
   Of that he showed,
   For you and me.

Money Cannot Bring Happiness

Money can't bring you happiness,
  With credit cards and debt,
  It can only bring you sleepless nights,
  And makes you worry and fret.

We shouldn't seek earthly things,
But seek God's Kingdom first,
For he will give us blessings and treasures,
That will not fit in your purse.

The treasures of earth can rust and fade,
But not so with treasures above,
For we will have blessings,
More than we can contain,
And covered in God's love.

God Sent the Holy Spirit

He called me into his banqueting table,
   And his banner over me is love,
He sends the Holy Spirit down,
As gentle as a dove.

He sent the spirit in tongues of fire,
Upon the upper room,
He took the frightened disciples,
And into stronger people,
He did groom.

With the power of the Spirit,
God is with us always,
We need not be scared or worried,
He is with us till the end of days.

He is the comforter that was promised,
The blessed trinity,
The Father, Son, and Holy Ghost,
For all eternity.

Two Paths

There are two paths in life,
The wrong and the right,
Follow the only way,
Keep Jesus in your sight.

Keep your eyes upon him,
And all else will grow dim,
The light of his radiance,
Will protect you from sin.

When you are tempted,
Whatever way that may be,
Remember W.W.J.D.
What would Jesus do if he were me?

Give Us Inspiration

Give us inspiration Lord,
To help us through the day,
When we get up and things go wrong,
Let us not be filled with dismay.

When we have hit rock bottom,
The only way is up,
We can always take comfort,
In the Eucharist,
And the cup.

We can always take comfort,
That whatever we go through,
We need never feel,
As though we're alone,
For we always will have you.

Through good times,
And bad times,
On you we can depend,
Our Father and mentor,
And also our best friend.

How Beautiful the Flowers Are

How beautiful the flowers are,
  But first they have to die,
  Before they can bloom again,
  Beneath the azure sky.

We also have to die to self,
  Before we can rise in Christ,
  The holy spotless Lamb of God,
  The ultimate sacrifice.

So we should put selfish thoughts away,
  And put our neighbours first,
  For there are many people out there,
  And for God's word they do thirst.

Go and spread the good news,
  There is hope for all mankind,
  Tell everyone you know,
  Make sure while there is time.

We Don't Need Designer Clothes

We don't need designer clothes,
 At an expensive price,
 We are clothed by the Lord,
 Who paid the ultimate sacrifice.

No amount of riches,
 Will get you Heaven bound,
 But only by trusting God alone,
 Can inner peace be found.

When we get to Heaven,
 The Lord will not say,
 "How much do you have in your bank?"
 "How much can you pay?"
 For us the price was paid that day,
 When he died upon Calvary's cross,
 And washed our sins away.

How Beautiful Are the Lilies

How beautiful are the lilies,
  How well fed,
  Are the birds of the air,
  They do not have a worry,
  They do not have a care.

If God can clothe,
And feed nature,
How much more,
We are to him,
For we should not fret or worry,
For worry can be a sin.

Worry is the devil's weapon,
It means we don't trust God,
It means we don't believe his word,
Or follow the way Jesus trod.

Always just remember,
Have faith in God alone,
And when you pray to Jesus,
Your petitions reach his throne.

Sometimes Life Is Unfair

Sometimes you think,
That life is unfair,
Where the wicked prosper,
And don't have a care.

Take heart,
And have faith in God,
Your Father and friend,
Whose power is omnipotent,
And loves without end.

He takes you out,
Of the miry clay,
And on a rock,
You will stand,
He will never leave you,
Or forsake you,
As he leads you by the hand.

So put your hand in his,
Who calmed the raging sea,
And you will feel,
Grace and mercy,
Descending on thee.

Life Is Like a Painting

Life is like a painting,
   With strokes added every day,
   If we put our trust in God,
   He will always lead the way,

Our Lord God is the artist,
With the brush firm in his hand,
And we cannot go wrong,
If we obey his command.

There may be little smudges,
When things go wrong throughout the day,
But don't give up,
Never give in,
For help is on the way.

With one touch of the brush,
Your life can turn,
From bad times into good,
And all the sins,
We have committed,
Will be washed,
In the Saviour's blood.

Don't Let the Sun Go Down on Your Anger

Never let the sun,
   Go down on your anger,
   Never hold a grudge,
   For your Father in Heaven,
   One day will be your judge.

If we cannot show forgiveness,
As Jesus told us to,
How can you expect him,
To forgive you.

Jesus left the great commandment,
Love others as yourself,
So love and respect,
Each others feelings,
And inside,
You'll feel better in health.

Holding a grudge,
Can eat away,
At your inner peace of mind,
It is far better show love and respect,
And to others be good and kind.

How Lovely It Is in the Summer

How lovely it is in the summer,
   When the sun shines warm and bright,
   When it rises early in the morn,
   And goes down late at night.
   Then comes the onset of winter,
   With the cold,
   The snow and ice,
   When all of nature,
   Goes to sleep,
   And the Earth,
   Does not seem quite as nice.

So it is with us,
When the sun shines in our lives,
All is well,
With the world,
And on happy vibes we thrive,
But when the winter darkness,
Blocks out our happy glow,
Just take heart,
And remember,
The sun will always,
Melt the snow.

When Your Burdens Grow Too Heavy

When your burdens grow too heavy,
   And your world around you falls,
When you feel so claustrophobic,
   And surrounded by four walls.
Just take your prayers to Jesus,
The walls he will take away,
And your burdens will be lightened,
And like bubbles float away.
Each one will burst and be no more,
Let him into your life,
He is knocking at the door.
Only you can say please enter,
Come into my life today,
For he is the only one,
The truth, the life, and the way.

You May Speak in Tongues

1 Cor. 13:1–13

You may speak in tongues of angels,
  Or have the gift of prophecy,
But without the gift of love,
  How useless they would be.

If you had faith to move mountains,
And gave everything to the poor,
Or sacrificed your body,
And tortures to endure,
Without the gift of love,
They are nothing worth,
Love is one of the most precious things on earth.

Love is patient,
Love is kind,
Let love fill your whole being,
Let love fill your whole mind,
Love takes away irritability,
And does not demand its own way,
So pray to God to fill you with love,
To help you through the day.

Love will last forever,
Forever it will endure,
It holds no count of wrongdoings,
It does not keep a score,
Remember faith, hope, and love,
These very important three,
But pray the Lord,
Will fill you with love,
For all his family.

When You Feel Like Job

When you feel like Job,
   And troubles surround,
You feel in chains,
   And your hands are bound.
Sing to the Lord,
   And praise his name,
Defeat the devil,
   And Jesus proclaim,
For he will help you,
   Whatever time of day,
You know he is listening,
   And to him you should pray.
Just like Job,
   You will receive God's blessings, too,
He will never turn his back on you,
   Even though at the time,
The sky seems black,
   Remember the Lord is always there,
And nothing shall you lack.
   He will bring you through,
And then you will feel,
   God's work in your life,
And his love he'll reveal.

Thank God in Times of Suffering

I thank you, Lord,
For my suffering and pain,
For the trials I have endured,
Again and again,
I have the choice,
The path to take,
Not to follow you,
Would be a mistake.
Though Satan may tempt me,
On my way,
"Leave me alone;
Get behind me," I say,
For all that I go through,
I know that you're there,
You know how I feel,
You are beyond compare.
You suffered like I did,
And even more,
Your death on the cross,
You had to endure,
But you did it for my sake,
And for the human race,
All so we could see you,
Face to face.

Dry Your Tears

Dry your tears,
And do not cry,
For the bad times will disappear,
And soon pass by.
In the distance,
There is a spark,
A hope and a light,
To shine in the dark,
It will shine,
To show the way,
To a wonderful, happier,
Brighter day,
The light will appear,
And then you will see,
What Jesus has planned,
Believe you me.
For every tear that's shed,
Will turn to joy,
So the Bible has said,
You may cry for a night,
But joy cometh in the morning,
So look to the light,
And the new day dawning.

The Phone Call

Sometimes we ring a person,
  On the telephone,
  The line is busy,
  Or the person's not at home.

Jesus's line is always open,
All you need to do,
Is put your hands together and pray,
He will always be there for you,
He is always ready to listen,
Be it day or night,
He is always ready to act,
And help us in our plight.

The receiver will never,
Be put down on you,
Or a silence down the other end,
For you can talk to Jesus,
Just like you talk to a friend.

God Has No Concept of Time

God has no concept of time,
In the blink of an eye,
A thousand years,
Or even two,
May have passed by.

We wait and wait,
And pray and pray,
And long and hope,
With faith,
For the day.
When our prayers,
Are not answered,
We do not see why,
We suffer and hurt,
And often cry.

But God in his wisdom,
Knows the way,
He sees the future,
And knows the right day,
To answer our prayers,
And then we will be filled,
With God's blessings,
And our hearts,
Will feel thrilled.

Every Cloud Has a Silver Lining

Each cloud has a silver lining,
However black they are,
You don't have to wait,
To make a wish,
By seeing a shooting star.

For we have all the answers,
We only need to pray,
And things will always get better,
However bad the day.

Our little cry of help to God,
His ears will hear our plea,
And he will always listen,
He will never forget thee.

Blue sky will appear,
And then from God above,
We will feel the warmth,
Of the suns rays,
The comfort of God's love.

Written On the Palm of God's Hand

Your name is written,
 On the palm of God's hand,
And no enemy or weapon,
 Against you will stand.
Your enemies shudder,
When they see God's power,
For he protects you every hour,
When you are awake,
Or when you sleep,
Safely in his arms,
He will keep.

He is our Father,
And through his son,
We can have a fresh start,
And a new life begun,
For his blood,
That was shed,
On that Good Friday morn,
Was the beginning,
Of a brand new dawn,
So the devil is defeated,
And so are our foes,
As our Lord God into battle,
Before us goes.

You Need a Firm Anchor

You need a firm anchor,
Through the rough sea of life,
You need a firm anchor,
In times of strife.
The anchor is God,
He is firm and sure,
And whatever you ask of him,
He will do even more.

He is generous and bounteous,
And gives all he can,
Look at the way,
He did not withhold his only son,
For the sake of sinful man.

He loves every one of us,
Whether we are good or bad,
And he hurts to see us,
Look forlorn and sad,
So when you are going,
Through a crisis,
And things get rather rough,
Just cling to God, the anchor,
And you will not feel scuffed.

We Look at the Sun and Moon

We look at the sun,
The moon and the stars above,
They tell of God's power,
They tell of God's love,
We in his image he did create,
Although Darwin's theory,
Many people debate.

Adam and Eve,
Were the first woman and man,
Who brought sin into the world,
But God had a plan,
He sent his son,
To shed his blood,
And there in our place he stood.

On his shoulders he took our sin,
And because of this act,
We are cleansed within,
He died for our sake,
So we could be free,
So we thank God every day,
For Calvary.

Hope

Hope means a word,
  That maybe it could,
Hope is a world,
That means it should,
But faith is a word,
That means we know,
That God will act,
His power to show.

For faith just grows,
As in God we trust,
It's not a case of maybe,
But know we must,
Put all our cares,
Into his hands,
And trust our Lord God,
Whose power commands,
All of the universe,
And all our fate,
So just trust in God,
Be patient and wait.

When You Are Having a Bad Day

When you're having,
  A really bad day,
  Just hold onto your dream,
  Just float away,
  To happier times,
  Then the sky will be blue,
  And things will turn out,
  Much better for you.

You know you can turn,
  To God to help you,
  Although you sometimes wonder,
  Why you are going through,
  This time of trouble,
  And time of trial,
  Just be patient,
  And wait awhile.

Don't give up,
  Just look at the sky,
  And see the clouds,
  As they float by,
  Just like the clouds,
  They will be gone,
  A rainbow will appear,
  And so will the sun.

He Will Fill Your Mouth with Laughter

Job 8:21

He will fill your mouth with laughter,
   And your lips with shouts of joy,
Just trust the Lord,
And his blessings you'll enjoy.

New every morning and every day,
God's blessings flow,
He will forever stay,
Right here beside you,
And within your heart,
He will never reject you,
And he will never depart,
For you are a child,
A child of his care,
And like any loving father,
He is always there.

When the Light Seems Dim

When the light in your life seems dim,
  And you are burdened down by sin,
  Just look unto the cross,
  Then life will not seem such a loss.

For the cross is where we look to,
  The sign of hope from above,
  For it's also the sign of suffering,
  And the sign of God's constant love.

It is on the wooden cross of Christ,
  That we can look and see,
  How Jesus died and suffered,
  And shed his blood for you and me.

The precious blood of Jesus,
  Was shed for the sake of our sin,
  So look unto the cross of Christ,
  And evermore thank him.

When the News Can Be Full of Gloom

When we look at the news,
　That is full of gloom,
As Christians,
Fear should have no room,
To spoil the life,
That God has given,
So with trust in God,
Fear shall be driven,
Out of our lives,
And forever gone,
As we trust in God,
And Jesus, his son.

Fear means we don't trust in God above,
Who sent his son,
Who out of love,
Died and rose that we could be,
Happy and content,
And from sin free.

So put your trust and faith in he,
Who walked the shores of Galilee,
And cares what happens in your life,
And hurts when you have cares and strife.

Let not fear have a part,
Within your life,
Or in your heart,
With faith and hope,
And trust in God,
Fear will be removed,
And underfoot trod.

Feeling Cold and Empty

Are you feeling cold and empty,
Sad and glum within?
Waiting for an answer to prayer,
Or wondering where to begin.
Just keep on praying,
And knocking at the door,
Then you will have the answer you need,
God's blessings and even more,
For God will not ignore you,
He is just waiting for the time to be right,
Just like to Joseph in prison,
He will show his power and might.
Just look what he went through,
Slavery, imprisonment and pain,
Then when God finally released him,
With Pharaoh he did reign.
It's all about right timing,
So leave it in God's hands,
And then you sill see why you had to wait,
And what the Master has already planned.

Say Good Morning

Say, "Good morning, Holy Spirit;
   Guide and empower me this day,
   Let your way be shown within my life,
   And help me not to stray."
   Although the worlds ways are full of temptation,
   We know that we should say no,
   So follow the way of Jesus,
   The only way to go.

The Spirit will lead you onwards,
   To places you have never been,
   And then around you,
   The beauty of Jesus will be seen.
   When trouble and temptation,
   Comes knocking at your door,
   The Holy Spirit will come to your aid,
   As he has many times before.

So say, "Good night, Holy Spirit,
   Thank you for the day,"
   And as I lay my head down to rest,
   I thank the Lord and pray.

I Believe

I believe that rainbows will always follow rain,
I believe that joy will always follow sorrow and pain,
I believe that God each day sends blessings from above,
I believe that God each day shows his constant love,
I believe that good will come out of bad,
I believe that Jesus is the best friend I ever had.
I believe that God sent down his blessed holy son,
To conquer death and evil,
The victory has been won.
I believe that through his death,
And shedding of his blood,
He took my sins and burdens,
And in my place he stood,
I believe that in Heaven there is a room for me,
I believe that one day face to face Jesus I will see.

When Creation Began

Through distant time,
   When creation began,
   And Adam was the only man,
   How wonderful it must have been,
   The world so new,
   So fresh and clean,
   No pollution, no war, just peace,
   Only the sound of nature,
   As it did increase,
   Until the serpent slithered away,
   Into the garden,
   And to this day,
   We pay the price of Adam's fall,
   But if we listen to God's call,
   And to his son who took our sin,
   And died so we could be with him,
   We will be redeemed, restored, forgiven,
   So at last we can take our place in Heaven.

Advent

This is the time of Advent,
 The coming of our King,
Who left his throne in Heaven,
Forgiveness and love to bring.
He is known as Emmanuel,
He is known as the Prince of Peace,
His reign will go on forever,
His Kingdom will never cease.

With four weeks to Christmas,
As around the shops we go,
With all the glitter and tinsel,
Let us not forget what we know,
That the true meaning of Christmas,
Is about the Saviour's birth,
And how over two thousand years ago,
He came to grace this earth.

Let us not forget how he humbled himself,
And became a servant King,
And let us with the angels in Heaven,
Forever his praises sing.
As we remember, he came as a baby,
But we know he will return again,
With his heavenly hosts of angels,
And forever he will reign.

Do You Ever Wonder

Do you ever wonder.
Why you are here on Earth?
And why at a particular time and place,
It wasn't just a coincidence,
That it happened to be your birth.
God has a plan for each woman and man,
The future we cannot see,
But if we trust in God above,
We will see it had to be.

Each person that we come across,
Each path that we do take,
Is all the Master's plan for you,
It is the choice you have to make.

So be sure you follow the right path,
The path that is narrow and straight,
And when you get to Heaven,
The Lord will open the gate.

As the Sunshine Melts the Snow

Like the sunshine melts the winter snow,
So Jesus can melt your heart,
And he will show,
How to love and forgive,
And how to receive his peace,
His wholesome *shalom*,
That will not cease.

All your bitterness and hate,
He will take away,
And replace it with love,
And mercy day by day,
So you will see others,
In a different light,
And even your enemies,
You will love,
Instead of want to fight.

The key to peace and happiness,
Is open your heart to the Lord,
Then you will be at peace with others,
And you will be of one accord.
He will melt bit by bit the bitterness,
The hatred and the pain,
Then you will never feel,
The same way again.

Chase the Clouds Away

Behind the clouds of black and grey,
  They will soon disperse for a better day,
And when life does not fulfil its dream,
And you feel as though you want to scream,
Just hold on and don't give up,
Even when life seems like a bitter cup,
For if you add a smile to make it sweet,
Life will seem better and more complete.
A smile will help you get through the day,
And will make you feel better in every way,
It cheers you up and gladdens your heart,
And chases negative feelings, that will soon depart.
A smile is so infectious,
A smile is soon spread around,
And people prefer a happy face,
Rather than a permanent frown.
So come on and be glad and be happy,
Try not to be blue and sad,
For if we look on the bright side of life,
Things will not seem quite as bad.

The Rainbow

When you see a rainbow arched across the sky,
   Have you ever wondered and asked the question, "Why?"
It all goes back to Noah's flood,
Before Christ redeemed us by his blood,
God showed that he would never again,
Destroy the earth by flood or rain.
For the rainbow is a covenant between mankind
      and God above,
To show he cares about us all,
As he showers us with his love,
His love will never falter,
His love will never fail,
His love is ever constant,
His love will not grow pale.
So the next time you see a rainbow,
In all its bright array,
Just remember God loves you,
And blesses you every day.

Free As a Bird

Free as a bird up in the sky,
  My heart skips a beat,
  I wonder why?
  I feel the love of my Lord within,
  Who died and cleansed me from my sin,
  I am free from worry,
  And free from fear,
  I know my Lord loves me,
  To him I am dear,
  For I know he died for the love of me,
  And laid down his life at Calvary.
  Before I was born and right through life,
  My Lord is with me in times of strife,
  I never ever feel alone,
  He is easier to contact that using a phone,
  For when I get bogged down with the cares of the day,
  I put my hands together and to God I pray.

Thoughts of Summer

How I long for the summer,
And the long, sunny days,
The heat on my body,
Of the warm sun's rays,
Chilling out on the beach,
Or by the pool,
Just diving in to keep myself cool,
Quaint little villages of pink, blue, and white,
Eating out in tavernas,
Dancing into the night.

No early mornings,
No thoughts of work,
Should we visit the pyramids of Egypt?
Or an old Scottish Kirk?
With brochure in hand,
I flick through the pages,
The choice is endless,
It seems to take ages,
To choose where to go and what to do,
The choice is entirely up to you.

The only thing that keeps me sane,
Through the long winter nights,
Through the snow and the rain,
Is the thoughts of the summer,
With all its joy and fun,
The long balmy nights,
And the hot summer sun.

Look at the Seasons

I look at the winter,
  With its flakes of snow,
I look at the oceans,
  And the creatures below,
I look at the mountains,
  And their mighty peaks,
Of God's power and love,
  To me it speaks.

I look at the spring,
  And the newborn lambs,
How God created it all,
  By his mighty hands,
The summer sun,
  And the sky of blue,
All speaks of God's mercy,
  To me and you.

I look a the autumn,
  All golden and brown,
And how God himself,
  To Earth came down,
The master of all,
  We survey and see,
Gave up his life at Calvary.

This shows how much he loves us so,
  And if you trust in him,
You will get to know,
  Your Lord and God,
As your personal friend,
  Whose love is forever,
And without end.

The Light of Christ

The light of Christ forever burning,
  Sinners in repentance turning,
  To the light that shows the way,
  And turns our darkness into day.
  We turn to Christ in times of trials,
  He turns our sadness into smiles,
  For he is the one and only light,
  That shines forever both day and night,
  For he is the light that cannot be put out,
  Read your Bible if you have any doubt.

  Although the world seems full of dark,
  Just look back at Noah's ark,
  For God keeps his promises,
  Right to this day,
  And he will never forget you,
  As to him you pray,
  For the light of the world,
  Will forever shine,
  As I am my Saviour's,
  And he is mine.

Spring

I look upon the fields of gold,
The daffodils proud heads they hold,
The birds in the trees,
Do sweetly sing,
To herald the beginning of wonderful spring.

All through the dark of winter,
All nature does sleep,
As the snow disappears,
The buds do peep,
And then they burst forth,
To a beautiful flower,
And are greeted by the sun,
And the April shower.

It is the beginning of hope anew,
All nature wakes to the morning dew,
The spider's webs upon the trees,
The humming of the passing bees,
The lambs in the field do skip and play,
To greet the beginning of another day.

How wonderful and fresh,
With grass now green,
Where once the snow and ice have been.
For God gives us the Seasons,
Spring, summer, winter and fall,
He is there all the time,
If only we call,
He is there to answer,
To us he will speak,
If only we listen,
His will to seek.

Winter

The rain comes down,
 The wind it moans,
It seeps right through into my bones,
I have to wear my winter attire,
And snuggle up beside the fire.
It only seems like a few weeks ago,
I was in the sun,
Now I walk in the snow.
The snow it is so crisp and white,
How silently it falls in the middle of the night.
I love the summer with skins healthy glow,
As out and about I like to go,
But in the winter by the fire I dream,
Of warmer days and walks by the stream,
Of happier times of holidays gone,
And how the sun it always shone,
Of lazy days beside the pool,
A long drink in my hand to keep me cool,
Now it's hot drinks to keep me warm,
To keep out the cold,
And the winter's storm,
But soon the spring will then come around,
And buds and flowers appear from the ground,
And then it leads to warmer days,
With the warmth of the sun,
And its pleasant rays.

Easter

It's Easter time,
The bells are ringing,
Choirs of angels forever singing,
"Glory to God's son, who came.
Spotless lamb for sinners slain."

You died upon a wooden cross,
To give me life,
Your own you lost.
Your sacred blood came flowing down,
Upon your head,
Thorns for a crown.

Then on that glorious Easter day.
When you washed all my sins away,
You rose victorious from the grave,
You shed your blood,
Mankind to save,
And now I will forever praise,
My Lord and Saviour,
All of my days.

Three Crosses

On a hill three crosses stood,
The middle one,
Stained by the blood,
Of Christ who died,
To set me free,
So that I can live eternally.

He went to Heaven to prepare a place,
So that I may see him,
Face to face,
And there to worship,
Around the throne,
With the saints and angels,
My brand-new home.

He bore the guilt,
He bore the shame,
In the book of life,
There is my name,
For he came and died for me,
The precious Lamb of Calvary.

For Easter is the time to rejoice,
As Christians we have made the choice,
To follow Christ,
Who came to save,
Who conquered death,
And rose from the grave.

Do You Ever Think of Christmas

Do you ever think of Christmas,
And what we celebrate,
The longed for Messiah had come,
No more time to wait.
The light of the world shone brightly,
Upon that Christmas morn,
When Jesus Christ, the King of Kings,
And Lord of all was born.

He came into the world so quietly,
No one knew of him,
Born in a humble stable,
To save the world from sin.
The angels told the shepherds,
Who quickly came to see,
The Saviour who came down to earth,
For the sake of you and me.

Now because of Christmas,
And more so Easter day,
Jesus opened up for us,
A gateway to Heaven one day,
So that not only at Christmas,
But more so Easter day, too,
We can celebrate Jesus, our Saviour,
Who died on a cross for you.

Christmas

Christmas bells and carols,
Children's eyes aglow,
Robins in the garden,
A sprinkling of snow.
Christmas trees with tinsel,
And some with lights that flash,
Late night Thursday shopping,
The last-minute dash.
Christmas cards are posted,
The presents given out,
Christmas can be stressful,
Of that there is no doubt.
But if we sit and think about,
The Holy Saviour's birth,
And truly mean good will to all men,
And peace throughout the earth.
How wonderful this world would be,
Not just on Christmas day,
We would live in peace and harmony,
A better world in every way.

The Ultimate Sacrifice

You paid the ultimate sacrifice,
  You shed your blood and tears,
  Although you were only on this earth,
  For thirty-three short years,
  You turned the whole world upside down,
  You showed us how to live,
  And even there upon the cross,
  You said, "Father, forgive."
  You were buried in a borrowed tomb,
  Until that Easter morn,
  When new hope, new life, and victory,
  At that time was born,
  Victory over evil,
  Victory over the grave,
  You left your home in Heaven,
  Us sinners here to save.
  So at this blessed Easter time,
  May you feel the peace of Christ within,
  Who loves each and every one of us,
  Regardless of our sin.

Angels

Guardian, guiding angels,
Although you cannot see,
Are there to protect and watch over us,
Each one of us will be,
Surrounded and enfolded,
Within their power and care,
And when we are in danger,
We know they are always there.

Although in life we feel alone,
And that our life seems bleak,
It is then that these angels,
With love and care they seek,
The lost and the lonely,
The people who feel so bad,
The people who are so much in despair,
And those that feel so sad.

The angels fill us with new hope,
And they are all around,
With the little tender words and deeds,
That in each other can be found,
They plant the seed, the thought, the word,
That we should do or say,
And help us cope when things are tough,
And help us through the day.